DISCIPLES CALLED
TO WITNESS
THE NEW EVANGELIZATION

*"But you will receive power when the holy Spirit comes upon you,
and you will be my witnesses . . . to the ends of the earth."*

—Acts 1:8

COMMITTEE ON EVANGELIZATION AND CATECHESIS

UNITED STATES CONFERENCE OF CATHOLIC BISHOPS
WASHINGTON, DC

Disciples Called to Witness: The New Evangelization was developed as a resource by the Committee on Evangelization and Catechesis of the United States Conference of Catholic Bishops (USCCB). It was reviewed by the committee chairman, Bishop David L. Ricken, and has been authorized for publication by the undersigned.

Msgr. Ronny E. Jenkins, JCD
General Secretary, USCCB

First printing, January 2013
ISBN 978-1-60137-386-1

TABLE OF CONTENTS

PREFACE

"'But you will receive power when the holy Spirit comes upon you, and you will be my witnesses in Jerusalem, throughout Judea and Samaria, and to the ends of the earth.' When he had said this, as they were looking on, he was lifted up, and a cloud took him from their sight. While they were looking intently at the sky as he was going, suddenly two men dressed in white garments stood beside them. They said, 'Men of Galilee, why are you standing there looking at the sky?'"

—Acts 1:8-11

C hrist commands us to be his witnesses to the ends of the earth. We are to proclaim his Good News to all people, everywhere and at all times. After Christ promises the disciples that the Holy Spirit will come upon them, he ascends into heaven. The disciples, rather than heeding Christ's command to be his witnesses, stare "intently at the sky." It takes "two men dressed in white garments" asking, "Men of Galilee, why are you . . . looking at the sky?" for the disciples to begin to realize the meaning of Christ's command (Acts 1:10-11).

How often do we fail to realize that we are called to be Christ's witnesses to the world? Do we realize that our Baptism, Confirmation, and reception of the Eucharist bestow on us the grace we need to be disciples? Are we like the disciples staring at the sky rather than inviting those around us to experience Christ's love and mercy through the Church? How often do we reach out to our missing brothers and sisters by inviting them to join us at Mass or by asking why they no longer feel welcomed at the Lord's Table? The answers to these questions underlie the evangelizing mission of the Church, especially in the call of the New Evangelization.

The New Evangelization seeks to invite modern man and culture into a relationship with Jesus Christ and his Church. The New Evangelization strives to engage our culture and to help us draw our inspiration from the Gospel. The New Evangelization calls all Catholics first to be evangelized and then in turn to evangelize. While it is directed to all people, the New Evangelization focuses specifically on those Christian communities that have Catholic roots but have "lost a living sense of the faith, or even no longer consider themselves members of the Church."[1]

---

1   John Paul II, *Redemptoris Missio* (RM) (Washington, DC: United States Conference of Catholic Bishops [USCCB], 1991), no. 33. (Also available online at *www.vatican. va/edocs/ENG0219/_INDEX.HTM.*)

The Committee on Evangelization and Catechesis seeks to take up the call of the New Evangelization with this resource. Diocesan bishops, eparchs, pastors, diocesan and parish staff, and indeed all Catholics will find this resource helpful in the creation of outreach efforts aimed at inviting and welcoming Catholics back to the Lord's Table. This resource discusses

- The call of the New Evangelization within our cultural context (Part I)
- The theological foundations of the New Evangelization (Part II)
- The importance of evangelization and personal conversion, or *metanoia* (Part III)
- Ideas on how to create a "culture of witness" (Part IV)
- Key Components of outreach programs for diocesan and parish-based evangelization programs (Part V)

PART I

CURRENT CULTURAL CONTEXT

"While he was still a long way off, his father caught sight of him, and was filled with compassion. He ran to his son, embraced him and kissed him."

—Lk 15:20

The Ministry of Jesus

Christ calls all people to himself. Throughout his public ministry, the Lord Jesus welcomed the stranger,[2] healed the sick,[3] offered forgiveness,[4] and expressed his eagerness to give rest to the weary and burdened.[5] How do we, today, follow the call and summons of Jesus to seek out the stranger, heal the sick, and welcome the weary? Jesus, in and through his Church, wants us to experience the urgent vigilance of the father of the prodigal son so that as we anxiously await the return of missing family and friends, we will be ready to run to greet and embrace them.

Our Current Situation

Today, through the ministry of the Church, Jesus continues to call all people to himself. It is estimated that only 23 percent of U.S. Catholics attend Mass each week.[6] Those 77 percent absent from the eucharistic feast each week are not strangers: they are our parents, siblings, spouses, children, and friends. According to a recent Center for Applied Research in the Apostolate (CARA) study, the most common reasons given by Catholics who do not regularly attend Mass are *not* related to controversial issues. The reasons given instead point to a gradual slipping away from the faith. Most Catholics stop attending Mass because they (1) have busy schedules or a lack of

2   Jn 4:4-42.

3   Mt 20:29-34.

4   Jn 8:1-10.

5   Mt 11:28.

6   Center for Applied Research in the Apostolate (CARA), "Sacraments Today: Belief and Practice among U.S. Catholics," CARA, *cara.georgetown.edu/sacraments.html* (accessed February 15, 2011).

time, (2) have family responsibilities, (3) have health problems or disabilities, (4) have conflicts with work, (5) do not believe missing Mass is a sin, or (6) believe that they are not very religious people.[7] In other words, many of our brothers and sisters have simply drifted away from the Church. This is due in part to the busyness of modern life and to a changing culture. There are also Catholics who attend Mass on a regular basis but who feel unconnected to the parish community. The reasons for not attending Mass highlighted in CARA's study also point to an increased secularization, materialism, and individualism.

Secularism influences all aspects of society, claiming religion is merely a private matter. Pope Benedict XVI has cautioned, "Any tendency to treat religion as a private matter must be resisted. Only when their faith permeates every aspect of their lives do Christians become truly open to the transforming power of the Gospel."[8] Materialism also presents an obstacle to Christ. The ability to acquire limitless goods and an overreliance on science create a false sense of hope that we alone can fulfill our deepest needs. However, without God, our deepest needs cannot be fulfilled. "Without God, who alone bestows upon us what we by ourselves cannot attain (cf. *Spe Salvi*, 31), our lives are ultimately empty. People need to be constantly reminded to cultivate a relationship with him who came that we might have life in abundance (cf. Jn 10:10)."[9] Individualism leads to harmful forms of freedom and autonomy. After all, "we were created as social beings who find fulfillment only in love for God and for our neighbor."[10] Our personal relationship with Christ does not hinder our participation in the community of believers—the Church.

In addition, there is an unsettling ignorance of the Eucharist as well as an erosion of Sunday as the Lord's Day dedicated to prayer and rest. The reasons that Catholics cite for missing Mass can be met and overcome by parishes that foster a welcoming environment for adolescents, young adults, singles, married couples, parents, families, the sick or disabled, and anyone who is no longer active in the faith. The means for fostering a welcoming environment is the New Evangelization. The New Evangelization places a special emphasis

---

7   CARA, "Missed Mass Chart of Sacraments Today: Belief and Practice among U.S. Catholics," CARA, *cara.georgetown.edu/missmass.jpg* (accessed February 15, 2011). For the detailed analysis of reasons why Catholics do not regularly attend Mass, please see "Sacraments Today: Belief and Practice among U.S. Catholics," CARA, *cara.georgetown.edu/sacraments.html*.

8   Benedict XVI, Address of the Celebration of Vespers and Meeting with the Bishops of the United States of America, *www.vatican.va/holy_father/benedict_xvi/speeches/2008/april/documents/hf_ben-xvi_spe_20080416_bishops-usa_en.html*.

9   Ibid.

10   Ibid.

on welcoming back to the Lord's Table all those who are absent, because they are greatly missed and needed to build up the Body of Christ.

The New Evangelization

The New Evangelization is a call to each person to deepen his or her own faith, have confidence in the Gospel, and possess a willingness to share the Gospel. It is a personal encounter with the person of Jesus, which brings peace and joy. The New Evangelization provides the lens through which people experience the Church and world around them.

The New Evangelization invites people to experience God's love and mercy through the sacraments, especially through the Eucharist and Penance and Reconciliation. Evangelization is the essence of the Church's identity: "The Church on earth is by its very nature missionary since, according to the plan of the Father, it has its origin in the mission of the Son and the holy Spirit."[11] Pope Paul VI reawakened the Church's evangelizing mission, Blessed John Paul II championed the call for the New Evangelization, and Pope Benedict XVI has reaffirmed the need for the New Evangelization. In *Go and Make Disciples: A National Plan and Strategy for Catholic Evangelization in the United States*, the Catholic bishops of the United States have expressed a sincere desire to invite all of God's children to their place in the Church: "We want to let our inactive brothers and sisters know that they always have a place in the Church and that we are hurt by their absence—as they are. . . . We want to help them see that, however they feel about the Church, we want to talk with them, share with them, and accept them as brothers and sisters."[12]

Positive Developments

Dioceses and parishes have already responded to the call of the New Evangelization by creating evangelization formation programs. This formation helps prepare parish leaders to initiate catechetical and reconciliation initiatives, which are meant to invite back to the faith and welcome our brothers and sisters who have been away. Sources of hope in the Church include diocesan and parish efforts to continually strengthen high school–level catechetical programs and to re-energize youth ministry programs and young adult ministries so as to reach these populations before they stop practicing the faith.

---

11   *Ad Gentes*, no. 2.

12   *Go and Make Disciples: A National Plan and Strategy for Catholic Evangelization in the United States* (Washington, DC: United States Conference of Catholic Bishops, 2002), no. 40.

Currently, dioceses focus their efforts on marriage preparation programs for young couples discerning marriage and on programs for couples becoming new parents. Diocesan and parish leaders also make an effort to welcome immigrants and attend to the needs of diverse groups. Opportunities to live the Gospel through concrete action, and thus to transform our culture, are numerous through advocacy and social justice ministries. Direct service opportunities frequently bring people back to the faith; this is especially true of young adults who value service projects. Many parishes offer not only Masses but also religious education, formation programs, and other pastoral services for cultural groups in their native languages. Additionally, new ecclesial movements and communities are flourishing, and they are eager to join dioceses and parishes in evangelization efforts.

Areas of Growth

Even though much has already been done to welcome our missing brothers and sisters back to the Lord's Table, there is still so much more that can be done. Catholics may desire to take on the call to evangelize but feel ill prepared to explain Church teachings. Some believe they lack the formation to be personal witnesses to Christ. Also, our brothers and sisters who have drifted away from the faith may be unable to vocalize why they stopped regularly attending Mass and parish activities, or they may not know with whom they can speak about why they left. Adolescents and young adults need active and engaging ministries and formation opportunities, including direct service.[13] Communication and attention to cultural differences need to be addressed in ministry with diverse groups. Cultural factors, including the lack of Masses and sacraments celebrated in languages other than English, also contribute to people slowly slipping away from the Church.

The task before the Church is to form Catholics who are willing to communicate and witness the faith to those who are no longer actively practicing. By taking up the call of the New Evangelization, we will do as St. Paul commands us: "Welcome one another, then, as Christ welcomed you."[14]

---

13 Statistics point to a median age of twenty-one when Catholics are more prone to stop practicing their faith. Please see "The Impact of Religious Switching and Secularization on the Estimated Size of the U.S. Adult Catholic Population," CARA, *cara.georgetown.edu/CARAServices/FRStats/Winter2008.pdf* (accessed February 15, 2011).
14 Rom 15:7.

PART II

HISTORICAL CONTEXT OF THE NEW EVANGELIZATION

"Go, therefore, and make disciples of all nations, baptizing them in the name of the Father, and of the Son, and of the holy Spirit."

—Mt 28:19

The Church's *ad gentes* ("to the world") mission given to her by Christ is the proclamation of the Good News to those who do not know him. The historical and social circumstances of the twentieth century prompted the Church to renew her mission to evangelize. This renewed vision of evangelization includes, as Pope Benedict XVI has stated, the challenge to "propose anew"[15] the Good News to all of the Christian faithful, most especially to those of the faithful who are absent from the Lord's Table.

Pope Paul VI's Call for Evangelization

Ten years after the close of the Second Vatican Council and a year after the 1974 Synod of Bishops, Pope Paul VI issued *Evangelii Nuntiandi*. Pope Paul VI stated that the Church "exists in order to evangelize, that is to say in order to preach and teach, to be the channel of the gift of grace, to reconcile sinners with God, and to perpetuate Christ's sacrifice in the Mass, which is the memorial of his death and glorious Resurrection."[16] *Evangelii Nuntiandi* describes the essential aspects of evangelization as well as its effects on the one evangelizing and the one being evangelized. The proclamation of the Kingdom of God and salvation for all people through Jesus Christ is at the very core of the Church's mission and the essential aspects of evangelization.[17] To evangelize, one bears witness to God's Revelation in Jesus through the Holy Spirit by living a life imbued with Christian virtues, by proclaiming

---

15 Benedict XVI, Homily of First Vespers on the Solemnity of the Holy Apostles Peter and Paul, *www.vatican.va/holy_father/benedict_xvi/homilies/2010/documents/ hf_ben-xvi_hom_20100628_vespri-pietro-paolo_en.html.*

16 Paul VI, *Evangelii Nuntiandi* (EN) (Washington, DC: USCCB, 1975), no. 14. (Also available online at *www.vatican.va/holy_father/paul_vi/apost_exhortations/documents/ hf_p-vi_exh_19751208_evangelii-nuntiandi_en.html.*)

17 Cf. EN, nos. 8-9.

unceasingly that salvation is offered to all people through the Paschal Mystery of Christ, and by preaching hope in God's love for us.[18] Pope Paul VI recognized that the first proclamation of the Good News is directed *ad gentes*. However, he also recognized the need for the evangelization of the baptized who no longer practice their faith.[19] He called upon the Church to evangelize these two groups, to invite them to a life of conversion, and to add new meaning to their life through the Paschal Mystery of Christ.

Blessed John Paul II and the New Evangelization

Blessed John Paul II renewed the call to all of the Christian faithful to evangelize in the spirit of the Second Vatican Council and Pope Paul VI. "No believer in Christ, no institution of the Church can avoid this supreme duty: to proclaim Christ to all peoples."[20] Blessed John Paul II made evangelization a focus of his pontificate and emphasized man's need to be evangelized by the Church. Evangelization occurs most effectively when the Church engages the culture of those she evangelizes. In 1983, he addressed the Catholic bishops of Latin America in Haiti and called for a New Evangelization: "The commemoration of the half millennium of evangelization will gain its full energy if it is a commitment, not to re-evangelize but to a New Evangelization, new in its ardor, methods and expression."[21] This marked the first time Blessed John Paul II used the term "New Evangelization" as the theological concept of proclaiming the Gospel anew to those already evangelized. He called for new "ardor, methods and expression" of evangelization, ones that engage the present-day culture and modern man. Blessed John Paul II, in the encyclical *Redemptoris Missio*, provided three circumstances in evangelization: (1) preaching to those who have never heard the Gospel (*ad gentes*), (2) preaching to those Christian communities where the Church is present and who have fervor in their faith, and (3) preaching to those Christian communities who have ancient roots but who "have lost a living sense of the faith, or even no longer consider themselves members of the Church, and live a life far removed from Christ and his Gospel. In this case what is needed is a 'new evangelization' or a 're-evangelization.'"[22]

---

18   Cf. EN, nos. 26-28.
19   See EN, nos. 52-53; 56-57.
20   RM, no. 3.
21   John Paul II, *Address to CELAM* (Opening Address of the 19th General Assembly of CELAM, March 9, 1983, Port-au-Prince, Haiti), *L'Osservatore Romano* English Edition 16/780 (April 18, 1983), no. 9.
22   RM, no. 33.

Blessed John Paul II alluded to the New Evangelization again in his opening address to the Catholic bishops of Latin America in Santo Domingo, Dominican Republic, as well as in *Crossing the Threshold of Hope*. Although Blessed John Paul II did not develop a full theological scheme of the New Evangelization, his writings reveal central themes of the New Evangelization, including the implementation of the call of the Second Vatican Council to proclaim the Good News of Christ by the engagement of the present culture and to accompany individuals on their journey from this life to eternal life. For Blessed John Paul II, evangelization must proclaim the Good News, which when appropriated into one's life, leads to conversion. This conversion provides a life of witness to the Good News and compels one to fulfill his or her vocation to the universal call of holiness. One's vocation to holiness is strengthened through the gifts of the Church, namely the grace of the sacraments, prayer, Scripture, and the Church's teachings and traditions.

Pope Benedict XVI and the Future of the New Evangelization

During his homily on the Solemnity of SS. Peter and Paul at the Basilica of St. Paul Outside the Walls on June 28, 2010, Pope Benedict XVI renewed the Church's call to the New Evangelization. Pope Benedict XVI called for the *riproporre* ("re-proposing") of the Gospel to those regions "still awaiting a first evangelization" and to those regions where the roots of Christianity are deep but that have experienced "a serious crisis" of faith due to secularization.[23] He clarified that the New Evangelization is new, not in its content but rather in its inner thrust; new in its methods that must correspond to the times; and new because it is necessary to proclaim the Gospel to those who have already heard it.[24] Pope Benedict XVI calls the Church to evangelize by entering into dialogue with modern culture and confronting the cultural crisis brought on by secularization. To aid the Church in re-proposing the faith to modern society, Pope Benedict XVI established the Pontifical Council for the Promotion of the New Evangelization on September 21, 2010, and proposed that the New Evangelization be the focus of the next Synod of Bishops.

When describing why he created a council for the promotion of the New Evangelization, Pope Benedict XVI stated that the mission of the Church has always remained the same, but the cultural contexts confronting man and the Church have changed. The council will help the Church understand the cultural contexts of the twenty-first century. Pope Benedict XVI noted that

---

23 Homily on the Solemnity of SS. Peter and Paul.
24 Ibid.

the Church is being challenged by "an abandonment of the faith—a phenomenon progressively more manifest in societies and cultures which for centuries seemed to be permeated by the Gospel."[25] He also outlined the modern cultural factors, such as secularism, that are contributing to the decline of the Christian identity in the world. Pope Benedict XVI has also indicated that the New Evangelization is not a single formula meant for all circumstances; first and foremost, it is a personal "profound experience of God."[26]

25   Benedict XVI, *Ubicumque et Semper*, *www.vatican.va/holy_father/benedict_xvi/apost_letters/documents/hf_ben-xvi_apl_20100921_ubicumque-et-semper_en.html*.
26   Ibid.

PART III

THE FOCUS OF THE NEW EVANGELIZATION

"Come to me, all you who labor and are burdened, and I will give you rest."

—Mt 11:28

Jesus grants all people rest and comfort from the burdens of this world. The rest and comfort of Christ comes from the hope offered by him: the hope of salvation and eternal life. The hope of salvation proclaimed in the Gospel transforms our lives with the promise of eternal life and comfort to the weary. "The Christian message was not only 'informative' but 'performative.' That means: the Gospel is not merely a communication of things that can be known—it is one that makes things happen and is life-changing. *The dark door of time, of the future, has been thrown open. The one who has hope lives differently; the one who hopes has been granted the gift of a new life"* [emphasis added].[27] Jesus Christ offers us new hope through a New Evangelization. Through the re-proposing of the Gospel, the Church seeks to comfort all those who are burdened by offering faith, hope, love, and the gift of new life in Christ.

Those Who Are Evangelized

The New Evangelization calls us to renew our faith so that we can share it with others. Before one can evangelize, one must be evangelized. A disciple of Christ must continually renew his or her faith. The disciple who then shares the faith is an evangelist. The Church is called to renew her faith in every age and at the same time proclaim it: "The Church is an evangelizer, but she begins by being evangelized herself. . . . This means that she has a constant need of being evangelized, if she wishes to retain freshness, vigor and strength in order to proclaim the Gospel."[28]

---

27 Benedict XVI, *On Christian Hope* (*Spe Salvi*) (Washington, DC: USCCB, 2007), no. 2. (Also available online at *www.vatican.va/holy_father/benedict_xvi/encyclicals/documents/hf_ben-xvi_enc_20071130_spe-salvi_en.html.*)

28 EN, no. 15.

With a renewed faith, the Church goes forth to share the faith. Given the current cultural context of our society, the Church is directing her evangelization efforts in a particular way to those members of the Body of Christ who are absent. In *Go and Make Disciples*, the Catholic bishops of the United States described in general terms some reasons that have contributed to Catholics who no longer actively participate in the life of the Church: "Some were never formed in the faith after their childhood. Some have drifted away because of one or another issue. Some feel alienated from the Church because of the way they perceive the Church or its teaching. Some have left because they were mistreated by church representatives."[29] These broad categories represent various reasons why our brothers and sisters are no longer involved in the life of the Church. These descriptions are meant to help bishops and diocesan and parish staff to better understand why our missing brothers and sisters have stopped coming to the Lord's Table, enabling the Church to be an agent of healing and reconciliation.

The Response of the New Evangelization to Today's World

Attention should also be paid to the cultural contexts and situations that our missing brothers and sisters face. Pope Benedict XVI described some of the contemporary situations confronting modern man, including secularism, globalization, social communications, the economy, scientific and technological research, and civic and political life. Many of these societal realities are positive, but when taken to the extreme, they can lead to disillusionment and weariness. For example, more people than ever before are able to participate in politics and enjoy political freedom, but current extreme political forces are also causing war, injustice, and the slow erosion of human rights, including religious freedom.[30] The disparity in economic development, while lifting some out of poverty, has also led to an inequitable distribution of goods as well as damage to God's creation, which adds to the plight of the poor. Secularism has led to a diminishing recognition of Sunday as the Lord's Day, a holy day of prayer and rest. "[The New Evangelization] involves . . . the proclamation and demonstration that the Christian faith is the only fully valid response

---

29   *Go and Make Disciples*, no. 39.
30   These factors enunciated by Pope Benedict XVI in *Ubicumque et Semper* are elaborated on in the *Lineamenta for the 2012 Synod*. Please see Synod of Bishops, *Lineamenta for the 2012 Synod: The New Evangelization for the Transmission of the Christian Faith*, www.vatican.va/roman_curia/synod/documents/rc_synod_doc_20110202_lineamenta-xiii-assembly_en.html.

to the problems and hopes that life poses to every person and society."[31] The New Evangelization offers hope. Our hope is not in a program or philosophy but in the person of Jesus Christ, who comforts those who are burdened.

Currently, there are numerous pastoral programs meant to encourage and support people in their journey back to the faith. However, for these programs to be effective, bishops, eparchs, pastors, catechists, and indeed all Catholics reaching out to our missing brothers and sisters must touch the lives of others, interact with them, and show them how the faith answers the deepest questions and enriches modern culture. Many might ask, "How do I touch people's lives? How do I interact with others in a spirit of love? How do I explain how the faith addresses modern concerns?" The Church has the resources to help. One such resource involves cultivating a culture of witness.

---

31 *National Directory for Catechesis* (NDC) (Washington, DC: USCCB, 2005), no 17.A.

PART IV

CULTURE OF WITNESS

*"I give you a new commandment: love one another. As I have loved
you, so you also should love one another. This is how all will know that
you are my disciples, if you have love for one another."*

—Jn 13:34-35

Christ teaches us how to evangelize, how to invite people into communion with him, and how to create a culture of witness: namely, through love. A Christian life lived with charity and faith is the most effective form of evangelization. Evangelization testifies to the transformative power of the Gospel and the mission of the Church to sanctify society, hand on the faith to future generations, strengthen the faith of her members, and renew the faith of those who have slipped away from the Church:

> "Modern man listens more willingly to witnesses than to teachers, and
> if he does listen to teachers, it is because they are witnesses." . . . It is
> therefore primarily by her conduct and by her life that the Church will
> evangelize the world, in other words, by her living witness of fidelity to
> the Lord Jesus—the witness of poverty and detachment, of freedom in
> the face of the powers of this world, in short, the witness of sanctity.[32]

The faithful become agents of evangelization through living witness and commitment to the Gospel. The everyday moments of one's life lived with Christian charity, faith, and hope provide witness to family members, friends, neighbors, colleagues, and others who have stopped actively participating in the life of the Church. This witness is essential for reaching others in today's modern world.

Conversion

The witness of Christians, whose lives are filled with the hope of Christ, opens the hearts and minds of those around them to Christ. This openness to Christ is a moment of conversion (*metanoia*). It is the moment in which a person's life is reoriented to Christ, when he or she—by grace—enters into a relationship with him and thus enters into a relationship with the community

---

32   EN, no. 41.

of believers, the Church. "The purpose of this [new] evangelization is to bring about faith and conversion to Christ. Faith involves a profound change of mind and heart, a change of life, a 'metanoia.'"[33]

The New Evangelization does not seek to invite people to experience only one moment of conversion but rather to experience the gradual and lifelong process of conversion: to draw all people into a deeper relationship with God, to participate in the sacramental life of the Church, to develop a mature conscience, to sustain one's faith through ongoing catechesis, and to integrate one's faith into all aspects of one's life.[34] The process of conversion and evangelization that accomplishes the objectives above must include the witness of the Church through her members in the everyday living out of the Gospel. In light of today's cultural contexts and situations, many struggle with how to create a culture of witness that will invite our missing brothers and sisters back to the Lord's Table. In the *National Directory for Catechesis*, the Catholic bishops of the United States have provided catechetical methodologies that foster and sustain an evangelizing culture of witness.

Methodologies

Catechetical methodologies are based on the proclamation of the faith from Sacred Scripture and Tradition and their application to human experience, or they are based on human experience examined in light of the Gospel and teachings of the Church.[35] These catechetical methods, though distinct, are complementary and should guide pastoral programs aimed at renewing the faith of all Catholics, including our missing brothers and sisters. For these methodologies and the programs based on them to be effective, they must be grounded in witness to the Gospel. This section explores the following methodologies:

- Discipleship
- A commitment to the Christian life
- Parish life
- The liturgical life of the Church: popular devotions and piety
- The Christian family
- Catechists and teachers of the faith
- Human experience

---

33 NDC, no. 17.A.
34 See NDC, no 17.A.
35 The first methodology is deductive, while the second is inductive. For a detailed examination of these two methods, please see NDC, no. 29.

Discipleship

To create a culture of witness, we must live explicit lives of discipleship. Being a disciple is a challenge. Fortunately, one does not become a disciple of Christ on his or her own initiative. The work of the Holy Spirit within the Christian community forms the person as a disciple of Christ. One seeking to learn how to be a disciple of Christ does so through apprenticeship. Those seeking to return to the faith are seeking to live a life of discipleship, to follow in the footsteps of Christ.[36] The parish must provide formed disciples who can accompany those who are returning to the Church and guide them throughout their journey. Apprenticeship "links an experienced Christian believer, or mentor, with one who seeks a deeper relationship with Christ and the Church."[37] Furthermore, this relationship is a "guided encounter with the entire Christian life, a journey toward conversion to Christ. It is a school for discipleship that promotes an authentic following of Christ based on the acceptance of one's baptismal responsibilities, the internalization of the word of God, and the transformation of the whole person to 'life in Christ.'"[38] Apprenticeship is an essential element in witnessing to the Gospel message.

A Commitment to the Christian Life

The commitment to living the Christian life provides an essential element of the culture of witness. To those seeking answers to the increasing secularization, individualism, and materialism of society, a Christian life provides a powerful witness to the Gospel. The public profession of one's faith through active participation in prayer, the sacraments, and especially Sunday Mass contributes to the sanctification of the world. Additionally, the works of charity and justice as well as the promotion of solidarity, justice, peace, and stewardship of creation build up the Kingdom of God.[39] Increasingly, we recognize that generosity of spirit and commitment to charity and justice are vehicles to bring people into relationship with Jesus and his Church. Social justice and direct service opportunities provide powerful experiences with the person of Jesus, especially for adolescents and young adults. Service, when understood as serving Christ in others and as a means to share the Gospel, has the ability to bring the server and the one being served closer to Christ.

---

36 NDC, no. 29.B.
37 NDC, no. 29.H.
38 NDC, no. 29.H.
39 NDC, no. 29.G.

Parish Life

Because the parish, through its pastor and members, is typically the first contact that returning Catholics have with the institutional Church, "it is the responsibility of both pastors and laity to ensure that those doors are always open."[40] Evangelization must remain rooted in the parish. It is in the parish that one becomes engaged with the Church community, learns how to become a disciple of Christ, is nurtured by Scripture, is nourished by the sacraments, and ultimately becomes an evangelizer. Successful evangelization and catechetical initiatives must be focused on the parish and parish life. The parish is where the faith is passed down, lived, and sustained for all members of the Body of Christ, most especially for those members seeking to return. "It is the responsibility of the parish community and its leadership to ensure that the faith it teaches, preaches, and celebrates is alive and that it is a true sign, for all who come in contact with it, that this truly is the living Body of Christ."[41]

The Liturgical Life of the Church: Popular Devotions and Piety

The active participation and practice of the liturgy, prayers, devotions, and popular piety of the Church provide a powerful witness to the faith. Participation in Mass should be encouraged, as the Eucharist is the heart of the Church's life. By participating in Mass, learning common prayers, and practicing devotions, a person appropriates the teachings of the faith. The prayers, popular devotions, and liturgies of the Church form the basis of "Catholic culture"; they allow for the community to pray together in a common language and contribute to one's continuing faith development.[42] Often, our returning brothers and sisters remember and have a fondness for their cultural and familial devotional practices. Asian and Pacific Islander and Hispanic devotions to our Blessed Mother, such as Our Lady of Antipolo and Our Lady of Guadalupe, should be encouraged. The use of gospel music by the African American community and liturgical movement by the black community should be fostered. The rich traditions of prayers, liturgy, and devotions such as *Akathistos*, *Paraklesis*, and *Molebens* of our Eastern Catholic Churches are a great grace and blessing. The desire of returning Catholics to reconnect with

---

40 USCCB, "Welcome and Justice for Persons with Disabilities: A Framework of Access and Inclusion," USCCB, *www.usccb.org/_cs_upload/8104_1.pdf* (accessed March 7, 2011).

41 NDC, no. 29.C.

42 NDC, no. 29.F.

their cultural devotional practices should be encouraged and fostered, as it presents an opportunity to invite them into a prayerful relationship with God.

The Christian Family

A culture of witness is sustained within the Church through marriage and the family. The communal relationship that exists between and among the three Persons of the Trinity is the model for Christian marriage,[43] and through the Sacrament of Matrimony, married love actually participates in Trinitarian love. It is within the Sacrament of Matrimony that the husband and wife evangelize, become evangelized, and share their witness of the faith to their children and to society. "Spouses 'not only receive the love of Christ and become a saved community, but they are also called upon to communicate Christ's love to their brethren, thus becoming a saved community' (cf. *Familiaris Consortio*, no. 49). The family founded on the Sacrament of Matrimony is a particular realization of the Church, saved and saving, evangelized and evangelizing community."[44]

The family, called the domestic Church,[45] is often the first place where one experiences and is formed in the faith. In fact, "the new evangelization depends largely on the domestic Church."[46] It is through the example of mothers and fathers, grandparents, siblings, and extended family members that one most concretely witnesses how to live a Christian life: "Family members learn more of the Christian life by observing each other's strengths or weaknesses than by formal instruction. Their shared wisdom and experience often constitute a compelling Christian witness."[47] It is vital that multiple generations, including grandparents, are engaged with the faith formation of younger family members. It is through the family that one journeying back to the faith can be awakened to, affirmed in, and encouraged by the love and mercy of Christ.

Catechists and Teachers of the Faith

The witness of catechists and teachers of the faith also creates and fosters a culture of witness. Catechists, together with the pastors of the Church,

---

43 NDC, no. 13.

44 Benedict XVI, Address to the Plenary Assembly of the Pontifical Council for the Family, *www.radiovaticana.org/en1/articolo.asp?c=542493* (accessed December 1, 2011).

45 USCCB, pastoral letter *Marriage: Love and Life in the Divine Plan* (Washington, DC: USCCB, 2009), 38-42.

46 Benedict XVI, Address to the Plenary Assembly of the Pontifical Council for the Family, *www.radiovaticana.org/en1/articolo.asp?c=542493* (accessed December 1, 2011).

47 NDC, no. 29.D.

are entrusted with the duties of teaching the faith, overseeing sacramental preparation, supporting the formation of consciences, and developing a love of prayer in those they catechize.[48] Catechists, who are dedicated disciples of Christ, provide a powerful witness to the Gospel. Additionally, Catholic schools and their teachers are witnesses to the faith. For over one hundred years, the Catholic school system in America has prepared generations of disciples in this country and been a powerful evangelizing presence. A vibrant Catholic identity and active promotion of gospel values in Catholic schools help foster future generations of disciples and evangelists.

Religious Experience

Discipleship is rooted in human experience. It is through human experience that one enters into a dialogue with modern culture. The human experience provides the "sensible signs" that help us come to know ourselves, one another, and God.[49] It is through common human experiences that the Word of God is revealed to us. These sensible signs are not abstract metaphysical signs but the concrete actions of the Holy Spirit present in the Christian's everyday life. These concrete actions of the Holy Spirit are numerous. Some common examples are retreats, direct service opportunities, parish prayer groups, Bible study programs, and involvement in the ecclesial movements. It is through the prompting of the Holy Spirit that one comes to understand the Good News of the Gospel. One's interaction with a Christian who lives an authentic gospel life leads to questioning about how to better appropriate the faith into one's own life. "Catechesis links human experience to the revealed word of God. . . . Catechesis helps them relate the Christian message to the most profound questions in life: the existence of God, the destiny of the human person, the origin and end of history, the truth about good and evil, the meaning of suffering and death, and so forth."[50]

These catechetical foundations are necessary for creating a culture of witness that testifies to the transformative power of the Gospel. The next section of this resource examines concrete skills and methods that can be used in diocesan and parish-based programs designed to invite our missing brothers and sisters back to the Lord's Table.

---

48 NDC, no. 29.E.
49 NDC, no. 29.A.
50 NDC, no. 29.A.

PART V

KEY COMPONENTS OF OUTREACH PROGRAMS

"Then Jesus said to them, 'Do not be afraid.'"

—Mt 28:10

Christ's message to the women at his tomb is also addressed to us. With his Passion, Death, Resurrection, and Ascension, Christ has vanquished death and granted us the hope of eternal salvation. Therefore, there is nothing to fear. However, because of Original Sin, we still experience fear and anxiety. Our brothers and sisters who no longer actively practice the faith may have apprehension about "coming back." They may wonder and worry about the following: Will the Mass be the same? Will I be judged because I stayed away so long? Maybe I have sinned so greatly that I cannot come back. What if I cannot remember the words to Mass?

Those who minister to our missing brothers and sisters are filled with questions also: Who am I to welcome people back? Am I actually capable of explaining what the Church teaches? Can I offer guidance and listen to their concerns without judgment? Indeed, Christians often experience these concerns when they evangelize. We are often afraid to ask our family, friends, and co-workers, "Would you like to come to Mass with me this weekend?" We have difficulty saying, "I saw the same news story, but this is what the Church actually teaches." We have trouble revealing, "Yes, sometimes going to confession is hard, but once I am there, I experience God's peace and mercy. If you haven't been in awhile, consider giving it another chance." There are several key components to successful evangelization programs designed to engage our missing brothers and sisters. This section of the resource will examine these components and offer concrete practices for fostering a culture of witness in diocesan and parish-based programs designed to invite all Catholics to a fuller participation in the life of the Church.

In 2010, the Committee on Evangelization and Catechesis conducted a nationwide survey of dioceses and eparchies on their best practices for outreach to Catholics. Based on the results of this survey as well as the *National Directory for Catechesis, Go and Make Disciples,* and *A Time to Listen . . . A Time to Heal: A Resource Directory for Reaching Out to Inactive Catholics,* the

Committee on Evangelization and Catechesis proposes several key components for programs meant to invite Catholics back to the Lord's Table.[51] These components are not meant to be comprehensive but rather serve as a foundation for diocesan and parish-based programs. The key components are the Holy Spirit and conversion, leadership, team preparation, an atmosphere of hospitality and trust, catechesis (including sacramental catechesis), prayer and popular piety, the Sunday Eucharist and effective preaching, resources, and continued support.

The Holy Spirit and Conversion

The New Evangelization is an opportunity for ongoing conversion. This reorientation of one's life toward Christ is possible because of the work of the Holy Spirit. The process of returning to active participation in the Church is a process of conversion that unfolds through the prompting of the Holy Spirit. For some Catholics, the conversion process to return to the Lord's Table will take time. Therefore, complete trust in the work of the Holy Spirit is essential. Programs designed to invite Catholics back to the Church should emphasize the following aspects of the role of the Holy Spirit and conversion:

- Openness to the Holy Spirit
- Personal witnessing to the role of the Holy Spirit in the lives of the pastor and team members
- Recognition that each person's conversion will be unique and unfold at a different pace
- Realization among team members that it was the Holy Spirit who led participants in their journey back to the Church (It is God who reaches out first.)
- Use of the Rite of Christian Initiation for Adults (RCIA) model for conversion
- Ability of the pastor and team leaders to articulate personal faith experiences
- Programs that are flexible, because some individuals may not be able to participate in an entire program
- Participation in retreats (e.g., marriage preparation and enrichment, adolescent, and young adult)
- Involvement in faith formation programs and direct service opportunities

---

51 For additional components and concrete practices, see *A Time to Listen . . . A Time to Heal*, 12-17 and *Go and Make Disciples*, nos. 90-127.

- Recognition that the conversion process may go beyond the length of the program and require follow-up with the person by a team member or pastor (All participants would benefit from follow-up contacts.)
- Evangelization and long-term evangelization planning in the parish

Leadership

The bishop, as the shepherd of his diocese and chief catechist, has been entrusted with the sacred duty to provide for the spiritual needs of those in his care, especially those who are absent from the community. The bishop's witness and active engagement in reaching out to our missing brothers and sisters demonstrates to the entire diocese the importance of this ministry. Pastors who assist the bishops in this sacred duty are vital elements in welcoming back our missing brothers and sisters. Lay parish leaders and staff also have a role in this ministry, as they are often the first points of contact and witness to the parish community. The following leadership skills and practices ought to be emphasized in outreach programs designed to welcome Catholics back to the Church:

- Public testimony and witness by the bishop about the importance of this ministry, including a personal invitation by the diocesan bishop to reconnect with one's parish
- Personal invitations to those who are missing to join the community for Sunday Mass
- Reaching out to former parishioners and demonstrating a spirit of welcome to all those who seek assistance
- Use of various ways to invite Catholics back (e.g., through letters, phone calls, social media, and home visits)
- Diocesan support of pastors and parishes implementing the bishop's pastoral plan for this ministry
- Support for pastors when engaging in and setting aside parish resources for this outreach
- Periodic parish censuses to determine the population and parish demographics (This is an opportunity to invite people to return to the Church.)
- Involvement of the clergy in the formation of lay leaders as evangelizers

Team Preparation

Programs that utilize a team-based approach should ensure that team members have been carefully selected and formed and that they embody a sense of welcome. Team members need not be master catechists, but they should have a deep love of the Church and a mature prayer life. If possible, the team should include Catholics who have had a lifetime commitment to the faith and others who have returned to the active practice of the faith. Some additional skills and practices for team formation include the following:

- A love of God and his Church
- Involvement and assistance of the pastor in the program
- Dedication to daily prayer
- Team members who are joyful mentors to returning Catholics
- Willingness to share one's own spiritual journey
- Ability to articulate how Christ changed one's life
- Knowledge to share the Gospel message
- Attendance at catechetical formation programs and retreats offered by the diocese or parish
- Participation in training programs for one-on-one evangelization, including online resources that make use of social media
- Ability to empathize
- Willingness to learn active listening skills
- Commitment to participate in the entire length of the program

An Atmosphere of Hospitality and Trust

The next element needed for effective evangelization is hospitality and trust. The entire parish community, especially the parish leadership, must foster a spirit of hospitality and welcome. This sense of hospitality extends beyond those who participate in formal "welcome back" programs. It includes Catholics who approach the Church at key "teachable moments," such as couples seeking the Sacrament of Matrimony, parents who have children in Catholic schools or parish-based religious education programs and are bringing their children for sacramental preparation, and Catholics who seek assistance from parish social ministry programs. Additionally, Catholics who choose to participate in a "welcome back" program ought to feel supported in their journey by the entire community. The following are among the other aspects of hospitality and trust that could be included in outreach programs:

- Fostering a liturgical environment that invites, spiritually fulfills, and welcomes the full and active participation of the parish
- Encouraging words of welcome by pastors at all liturgies, especially key liturgical moments when Catholics attend liturgies, such as weddings, funerals, quinceañeras, and Christmas and Easter Masses

- Offering the Sacrament of Penance and Reconciliation during hours that are convenient for those with busy work schedules, such as during lunch and after work
- The use of multiple languages in every aspect of parish life when culturally diverse groups are members of the parish
- Accessibility of worship and inclusion in all aspects of parish life for all, especially those with physical and mental disabilities
- Creation and pastoral formation of a welcome committee to help greet and support new parish members
- Parish-based support groups for those populations who tend to drift away from the Church, such as young adults, the newly married, new parents, and the recently divorced or widowed
- Openness to the participant's questions and listening to the group's concerns
- Respectful dialogue during the meeting sessions
- Confidentiality of conversations that take place during formation opportunities

Catechesis, Including Sacramental Catechesis

Many times, Catholics who have been away from the Church return with questions about the Mass, Scripture, and the teachings and traditions of the Church. These questions should be addressed openly and honestly by pastors and knowledgeable team members. Participants should be encouraged to ask questions, learn more about the faith, and receive the Sacraments of the Eucharist and Penance and Reconciliation to experience God's grace and mercy. The catechetical component should include the following elements:

- Teaching and reflections on the Creed, sacraments, and moral teachings of the Church based on the *Catechism of the Catholic Church* and the *United States Catholic Catechism for Adults*
- Bible study and reflection on the role of Scripture in one's life
- Opportunities for more thorough scriptural studies
- Sacramental catechesis on the Seven Sacraments, especially the Eucharist and Penance and Reconciliation
- Encouraging returning Catholics to receive the Sacraments of Penance and Reconciliation and the Eucharist
- Emphasis on the transformative grace of the Eucharist, including a sense of discipleship
- Links on the parish website to creditable Catholic catechetical websites and Catholic social media sites

- Use of teachable moments (e.g., Christmas, Easter, Baptism, First Communion, and other special liturgies) when Catholics come in contact with the Church (These are important opportunities not only for catechesis but also for evangelization.)
- Information about parish adult faith formation programs

Prayer and Popular Piety

Outreach programs must include prayer and help nurture the spiritual life of those returning to the Church. Even if someone has been away from the Church and Sunday Mass for a significant period of time, it should not be assumed that they have ceased praying. Indeed, many Catholics who have slipped away still have a deep devotion to Mary, the saints, and popular piety practices. These devotions should provide the basis for deepening their spiritual life. Programs developed for reaching out to our missing brothers and sisters should emphasize the following teachings and practices:

- Because prayer is the means through which we enter into a relationship with God, what a regular prayer life entails and how to pray each day should be explained.
- The Mass is the source and summit of the Church's life because it is through the Eucharist that one is nurtured by the Body and Blood of Christ.[52]
- The common prayers of the Church (Our Father; Hail Mary; Glory Be; Acts of Hope, Faith, Love, and Contrition) should be taught, explained, and prayed.
- The various expressions of prayer (vocal, meditative, and contemplative) along with the basic types of prayers (adoration, petition, intercession, thanksgiving, and praise) should be examined.[53]
- The rich spiritual traditions of the Church (Rosary, lectio divina, Liturgy of the Hours, novenas) should be explored.[54]
- Popular piety practices and devotions (devotion to the saints, scapulars, house blessings, home altars) should be taught and encouraged.
- The popular cultural devotions of various ethnic communities represented in the parish should be incorporated in various aspects of parish life.
- Ecclesial movements may be involved in parish life and faith formation.

---

52   See Lumen Gentium, no. 11.
53   See USCCB, United States Catholic Catechism for Adults (USCCA) (Washington, DC: USCCB, 2006), 467-468, 473-475.
54   See USCCA, 472.

The Sunday Eucharist and Effective Preaching

Outreach programs ought to invite people to return to the Sunday Eucharist. It is during this celebration that we encounter Jesus in the Eucharist. Pastors endeavor to ensure that both the preaching and the assembly are sensitive and welcoming to those who infrequently attend the Eucharist. The following are among the other aspects of the Sunday Eucharist and preaching that should be emphasized:

- Prayerful and faith-filled celebrations of the Eucharist with thoughtfully prepared homilies that stir the heart and mind
- The celebration of Sunday Mass in multiple languages when culturally diverse populations are present
- The accessibility of the Church building for those with disabilities, including the use of American Sign Language for the Deaf community
- A welcoming and inviting atmosphere toward those who infrequently attend
- Homiletic training during clergy formation and ongoing training for ordained clergy
- Opportunities for the clergy to study and reflect on Scripture
- Dedicated time for clergy for prayer and homily preparation
- Focus on integrating the teachings of the *Catechism* with Scripture in preaching

Resources

Catholics returning to the faith may need resources beyond what a team can provide. Team members will also need resources and support from the parish. Additionally, the community will need to commit parish resources to the program. The following resources should be readily available before a program begins:

- Meeting space in the parish that is set aside for the program
- A program budget for supplies, such as catechetical materials and refreshments
- Catechetical materials for team members so that they can better explain the Church's teachings
- Contact information for professionals who can assist those struggling with depression, addiction, or other related needs
- Contact information for the diocesan tribunal to assist those who wish to regularize their marriage

Continued Support

An evangelization program for returning Catholics is the first step in the process of rejoining the community at the Lord's Table. The Church's outreach cannot end with the completion of a program, no matter how good the program is. The Church's outreach cannot end upon one's return to Sunday Mass. We are called to continually support and encourage our returning brothers and sisters so that they can become true disciples of Christ. Continued support should include the following:

- An ongoing relationship between the participants and team members
- Encouragement to join parish prayer groups and small faith communities
- Opportunities for lifelong faith formation and catechesis, including reflection on Scripture
- Catechetical formation through parish and diocesan programs, including online formation programs
- Occasions for service within the parish community (e.g., to the sick and homebound)
- Involvement of ecclesial movements and new communities
- Parish revivals and missions
- Continued hospitality at parish liturgies and events

Dioceses, eparchies, and parishes are encouraged to use this resource to develop their own programs or enhance existing ones to "re-propose" the Gospel to our missing brothers and sisters. Outreach to Catholics seeking to more fully participate in the life of the Church is dependent upon the entire community's commitment to the New Evangelization.

CONCLUSION

"You will be my witnesses . . . to the ends of the earth."

—Acts 1:8

Through our Baptism, we become witnesses to the Gospel and disciples of Christ. As disciples and witnesses, we are called to ongoing conversion. To become evangelizers, we must first be evangelized. If we truly believe in the Gospel, then as a Church, we must take seriously Christ's commandment to "go, therefore, and make disciples of all nations, baptizing them in the name of the Father, and of the Son, and of the holy Spirit, teaching them to observe all that I have commanded you."[55] We bring the Good News to all people and nations, including those who have never heard of Christ, those who are no longer actively practicing their faith, and all those who are fervent in the faith. The New Evangelization challenges us to "re-propose" the Gospel to our missing brothers and sisters—those members of the Body of Christ who have drifted away from the Lord's Table.

The purpose of this resource is to encourage and assist diocesan and eparchial bishops and their pastoral leaders in their outreach efforts to engage our missing brothers and sisters. As the Church prepares for the 2012 Synod on the New Evangelization, new material will be added to the online version of this resource (*www.usccb.org/beliefs-and-teachings/how-we-teach/new-evangelization/disciples-called-to-witness/*). Each diocese, eparchy, and parish will implement this document in the manner most suited to its needs. Some will create door-to-door programs, use social media, develop printed resources, participate in local or national programs, or engage in a combination of all these activities. As dioceses and parishes begin preparations to create or renew their outreach to our missing brothers and sisters, it is important to remember that the New Evangelization is "primarily a spiritual activity."[56] We are called to invite our missing brothers and sisters back to life in the Church—a life in which we all experience God's love and mercy through the community of faith, nurture our spiritual lives through the sacraments and prayer, and are formed into true disciples of Christ.

---

55   Mt 28:19-20.

56   *Lineamenta*, no. 5.

PARISH REFLECTION QUESTIONS

Diocesan and parish leadership are encouraged to reflect on the following questions as they prepare pastoral plans aimed at "re-proposing" Christ to the faithful and inviting our brothers and sisters to the Lord's Table:

- How does the parish community provide people with opportunities for a personal encounter with Jesus Christ?
- In addition to offering sound catechetical instruction in the teachings of the Church, to what extent do faith formation programs have as an objective fostering a personal relationship with Christ?
- What does the parish do to help people deepen their prayer life?
- How has the parish recruited, formed, and supported individuals to be evangelizers through the witness of their lives?
- How are pastors fostering the consciousness of the laity to be evangelizers in the modern world?
- How do pastors engage people during "teachable moments," such as Baptisms, weddings, and funerals?
- Are there faith formation programs on how to pass down the faith for parents, grandparents, and godparents?
- Are there faith formation programs for adolescents and young adults on how to share their faith with others in college and in the workplace?
- How are pastors supported in their vocation to evangelize?
- Are there ongoing faith formation programs for pastors on homiletics?
- Is there instruction for pastors and parish leaders on how to use social media to reach people?
- What parish-based pastoral programs support people in their everyday lives? Are there programs for the newly married, new parents, divorced, grieving, and unemployed?
- How has the diocese and parish promoted the New Evangelization?

PRAYER FOR THE NEW EVANGELIZATION

Gracious and merciful God, we pray that through the
Holy Spirit all Catholics may hear the call of the New
Evangelization and seek a deeper relationship with your
Son, Jesus.

We pray that the New Evangelization will renew the
Church, inspiring all Catholics to "go forth and make
disciples of all nations" and transform society through the
power of the Gospel.

We pray for all members of the Church, that we heed the
words of Christ—"do not be afraid"—and, strengthened by
the Holy Spirit's gift of courage, give witness to the Gospel
and share our faith with others.

We pray that we may become like the father of the prodigal
son—filled with compassion for our missing brothers and
sisters—and run to embrace them upon their return.

We pray that all people yearning to know Christ and the
Church may encounter him through the faithful who
witness to his love in their lives.

Loving God, our Father, strengthen us to become witnesses
to the saving grace of your Son, Jesus, our Lord, who lives
and reigns with you, in the unity of the Holy Spirit, one
God, for ever and ever.

Amen.

ADDITIONAL RESOURCES

Please visit the New Evangelization website (*www.usccb.org/beliefs-and-teachings/ how-we-teach/new-evangelization*) for more interactive resources, including prayers, cultural diversity practices, marriage and family life information, and numerous catechetical tools. The documents and other materials listed in this section focus on evangelization and catechesis.

Second Vatican Council Documents on Catechesis and Evangelization:

- *Decree on the Apostolate of the Laity* (*Apostolicam Actuositatem*). Teachings on the baptismal vocation of the lay Christian faithful in the Church and the world. *www.vatican.va/archive/hist_councils/ii_vatican_council/documents/vat-ii_decree_19651118_apostolicam-actuositatem_en.html*
- *Dogmatic Constitution on the Church* (*Lumen Gentium*). The Council's teaching on the nature of the Church and the universal call of holiness. *www.vatican.va/archive/hist_councils/ii_vatican_council/documents/vat-ii_const_19641121_lumen-gentium_en.html*
- *On the Mission Activity of the Church* (*Ad Gentes*). The Council's teaching on the missionary vocation of the Church. *www.vatican.va/archive/hist_councils/ii_vatican_council/documents/vat-ii_decree_19651207_ad-gentes_en.html*

Vatican Documents on Catechesis

- *Catechism of the Catholic Church.* The official *Catechism* of the Universal Church that serves as a point of reference for all regarding the faith and morals of the Church. *www.usccb.org/beliefs-and-teachings/what-we-believe/catechism/catechism-of-the-catholic-church/*
- *Compendium of the Catechism of the Catholic Church.* The *Compendium* contains, in a concise manner, all the Catholic Church's teachings on faith and morals as found in the *Catechism.* *www.vatican.va/archive/compendium_ccc/documents/archive_2005_compendium-ccc_en.html*
- *General Directory for Catechesis.* The *Directory* presents both the content and methods for handing on the faith through catechesis. *www.vatican.va/roman_curia/congregations/cclergy/documents/rc_con_ccatheduc_doc_17041998_directory-for-catechesis_en.html*

Vatican Documents on Evangelization

- *Address to the Plenary Assembly of the Pontifical Council for the Family.* A message from Pope Benedict XVI on family life and the New Evangelization. *www.radiovaticana.org/en1/articolo.asp?c=542493*
- *God Is Love (Deus Caritas Est).* Pope Benedict XVI's encyclical on Christian love. *www.vatican.va/holy_father/benedict_xvi/encyclicals/documents/hf_ben-xvi_enc_20051225_deus-caritas-est_en.html*
- *Lineamenta for the 2012 Synod: New Evangelization for the Transmission of the Christian Faith.* The working document of the 2012 Synod Fathers that begins to examine the possible discussion topics at the Synod on the New Evangelization. *www.vatican.va/roman_curia/synod/documents/rc_synod_doc_20110202_lineamenta-xiii-assembly_en.html*
- *Message for the 2012 World Day of Migrants and Refugees.* A message from Pope Benedict XVI on migration and the New Evangelization. *www.vatican.va/holy_father/benedict_xvi/messages/migration/documents/hf_ben-xvi_mes_20110921_world-migrants-day_en.html*
- *On Christian Hope (Spe Salvi).* Pope Benedict XVI's encyclical on the theological virtue of hope. *www.vatican.va/holy_father/benedict_xvi/encyclicals/documents/hf_ben-xvi_enc_20071130_spe-salvi_en.html*
- *On Evangelization in the Modern World (Evangelii Nuntiandi).* Pope Paul VI's letter on preaching the Gospel and sharing the faith in the modern world. *www.vatican.va/holy_father/paul_vi/apost_exhortations/documents/hf_p-vi_exh_19751208_evangelii-nuntiandi_en.html*
- *On the Permanent Validity of the Church's Missionary Mandate (Redemptoris Missio).* Blessed John Paul II's encyclical on the nature of the Church's mandate to spread the Gospel and his urgent call to all Christians to participate in missionary activities. *www.vatican.va/holy_father/john_paul_ii/encyclicals/index.htm*
- *The Door of Faith (Porta Fidei).* The Announcement of the Year of Faith, October 11, 2012–November 24, 2013. *www.vatican.va/holy_father/benedict_xvi/motu_proprio/documents/hf_ben-xvi_motu-proprio_20111011_porta-fidei_en.html*
- *The Lord's Day (Dies Domini).* Blessed John Paul II's letter on keeping the Lord's Day holy. *www.vatican.va/holy_father/john_paul_ii/apost_letters/documents/hf_jp-ii_apl_05071998_dies-domini_en.html*
- *The Word of the Lord (Verbum Domini).* The post-synodal document on the Word of God in the life and mission of the Church. *www.vatican.va/holy_father/benedict_xvi/apost_exhortations/documents/hf_ben-xvi_exh_20100930_verbum-domini_en.html*

United States Conference of Catholic Bishops Documents on Evangelization and Catechesis

- *A Time to Listen . . . A Time to Heal: A Resource Directory for Reaching Out to Inactive Catholics.* Washington, DC: USCCB, 2002.
- *Empowered by the Spirit: Campus Ministry Faces the Future.* old.usccb.org/education/highered/empowered.shtml
- *Go and Make Disciples: A National Plan and Strategy for Catholic Evangelization in the United States.* www.usccb.org/beliefs-and-teachings/how-we-teach/evangelization/go-and-make-disciples/go-and-make-disciples-a-national-plan-and-strategy-for-catholic-evangelization-in-the-united-states.cfm
- *National Directory for Catechesis.* Washington, DC: USCCB, 2005.
- *Sons and Daughters of the Light: A Pastoral Plan for Young Adult Ministry.* Washington, DC: USCCB, 2010.
- *Renewing the Vision: A Framework for Catholic Youth Ministry.* Washington, DC: USCCB, 2002.
- *Teaching the Spirit of Mission Ad Gentes: Continuing Pentecost Today.* www.usccb.org/beliefs-and-teachings/what-we-believe/teaching-the-spirit-of-mission-ad-gentes-continuing-pentecost-today.cfm
- *The Hispanic Presence in the New Evangelization in the United States.* Washington, DC: USCCB, 1996.
- *To the Ends of the Earth: A Pastoral Statement on World Mission.* old.usccb.org/wm/earth.shtml
- *What We Have Seen and Heard: A Pastoral Letter on Evangelization from the Black Bishops of the United States.* Washington, DC: USCCB, 1984.

Diocesan Evangelization Resources

The following list represents a sampling of diocesan resources. All diocesan websites are available at *www.usccb.org/about/bishops-and-dioceses/all-dioceses.cfm.*

Selected Diocesan Evangelization Documents

- Bishop Robert J. Carlson, Pastoral Letter on Evangelization. *saginawdiocese.samsa.com/images/Pastoral_Evangelization_010608.pdf*
- Bishop Nicholas DiMarzio, "Do Not Be Afraid": A Pastoral Vision for the New Evangelization. *development.dioceseofbrooklyn.org/about/dont_be_affraid_english.aspx*

- Bishop Paul D. Etienne, A Pastoral Plan for Holiness of Life for the People of God of the Diocese of Cheyenne. *www.dioceseofcheyenne.org/pdfs/BishopPastoralLetter.pdf*
- Bishop José H. Gomez, You Will Be My Witnesses: A Pastoral Letter to the People of God of San Antonio on the Christian Mission to Evangelize and Proclaim Jesus Christ. *www.archsa.org/documents/anv_en.pdf*
- Bishop William E. Lori, Praying for a New Pentecost: A Pastoral Letter on Evangelization. *www.bridgeportdiocese.com/index.php/ourbishop/article/pastoral_letter_2001_05*
- Bishop David L. Ricken, Parishes Called to Be Holy, Fully Engaged, Fully Alive: A Pastoral Letter on Priorities for Parishes and the Diocese. *www.gbdioc.org/images/stories/Main_Links/Who_we_are/Bishops/pdf/2011-Pastoral-Letter_06-02-2011.pdf*
- Cardinal Donald W. Wuerl, Disciples of the Lord: Sharing the Vision. A Pastoral Letter on the New Evangelization. *www.adw.org/pastoral/eletterlink.asp*

Selected Diocesan Evangelization Websites

- Chicago, IL: *www.wearemissionary.org*
- Cincinnati, OH: *www.catholiccincinnati.org/ministries-offices/evangelization-and-catechesis*
- Green Bay, WI: *www.gbdioc.org/evangelization-a-worship/spirituality-and-evangelization.html*
- Houma-Thibodaux, LA: *www.htdiocese.org/OfficeofNewEvangelization/tabid/607/Default.aspx*
- Philadelphia, PA: *archphila.org/evangelization/formlaity/parish_evangelization/parish_evangelization.htm*
- Portland, ME: *www.portlanddiocese.org/info.php?info_id=93*
- St. Petersburg, FL: *home.catholicweb.com/dosp_elff*
- San Antonio, TX: *www.archsa.org/evangelization/about.aspx*
- Seattle, WA: *www.seattlearchdiocese.org/CFF/CatholicsComeHome.aspx*
- Washington, DC: *site.adw.org/archdiocese-of-washington-living-the-new-evangelization*